NATIONAL DEFENSE UNIVERSITY

JOINT FORCES STAFF COLLEGE

JOINT ADVANCED WARFIGHTING SCHOOL

TO STAY OR NOT TO STAY: NON-COMBATANT EVACUATION OPERATIONS AND THEIR IMPACT ON HOST NATION/REGIONAL STABILITY

by

Stephen M. Kampen

Lieutenant Colonel, United States Marine Corps

ABSTRACT

The United States Ambassadors and Geographic Combatant Commanders are responsible for protection of United States citizens in their respective areas of responsibility. Accordingly, planning and practicing of procedures for Non-combatant Evacuation Operations (NEOs) are prudent and necessary especially as stability, in a Host Nation or region, waivers: however, the decision to make necessary preparations for an evacuation may in fact precipitate the requirement to execute one, thus framing an undesirable decision to evacuate.

The current fiscal constraints coupled with a future security environment characterized by complexity, uncertainty and rapid change require evaluation of past evacuations up to and including military assisted evacuations or NEOs. These lessons can inform future leaders as they consider how to best utilize the unique characteristics of the Departments of State and Defense to safeguard American Citizens abroad.

CONTENTS

CHAPTER 1

INTRODUCTION

Noncombatant Evacuation Operations (NEOs) are military operations executed at the request of and led by the Department of State in order to remove American citizens and other designated personnel from a host nation where the security environment is no longer at a level in which their safety can be ensured. The Department of State has conducted numerous drawdowns of personnel from host nations without the assistance of the Department of Defense and has only requested support from the Department of Defense on a handful of occasions. What has led to so few NEOs actually occurring? The following hypothetical scenario will illustrate potential decision points that when made could influence the escalation or de-escalation of the impending crisis. In this context of a plausible, worst-case scenario of a war on the Korean Peninsula, NEO is a serious challenge.

In the not too distant future, regional tensions are likely to continue to escalate as the People's Republic of China continues to assert expanded territorial rights over the Spratly Islands, Scarborough Shoals, and the Diaoyu/Senkaku Islands. These challenges over the disputed rights of all the neighboring nations have drawn the global community, to include the United States and United Nations, to call for peaceful diplomatic resolutions to the conflicted claims. Japan, Taiwan, Vietnam, Malaysia, Philippines and Brunei have continued to assert their territorial claims which have resulted in several small scale military confrontations. These confrontations could result in escalations of military force that could envelop the region in conflict.

Adding to the potential turmoil across the globe, in the Middle East, Iran continues to flaunt the international agreements they have made to enrich uranium for their nuclear program. Israel has continued to warn the international community that it is prepared to ensure that Iran does not possess a nuclear weapon and has demonstrated its resolve by executing a surprise air raid to neutralize their nuclear production facilities. Continued aggressive moves by Russia, after the successful annexation of Crimea from the Ukraine, have led to rising tensions in the region as well.

In the United States, budget constraints and sequestration avoidance remain a concern as the administration and Congress manage the budget process. This has forced the Defense Department to continue on its path of downsizing. Both the Army and Marine Corps will have reduced personnel strength to numbers that have not been seen since pre-World War II and pre 9/11 levels respectively. Additionally, the United States has completed its withdrawal from Afghanistan after the longest combat troop commitment in United States history.

Against this backdrop of significant domestic and global turmoil, the Kim Jung Un regime in the Democratic People's Republic of Korea (DPRK) launches a surprise air, missile and ground assault across the 38th Parallel. DPRK forces rapidly gain momentum and achieve initial success in their invasion due to the surprise achieved. In another possible scenario, against the similar backdrop, the DPRK begins to show signs of increasing military readiness along the border. As a result of the increasing tensions on the Korean Peninsula the United States Government authorizes non-essential civilians to evacuate the Republic of Korea (ROK). As this step is announced and begun to execute the DPRK makes the decision to order an all-out attack on the ROK.

Although hypothetical scenarios that could be deemed worst case, the challenges that are addressed are currently being dealt with and are plausible. What is the United States to do in such an event? Do you remove the non-combatants from the theater if you have time or do they remain and shelter in place? This question probably kept many senior leaders up at night during the Cold War. However, the challenges of the Pacific Theater, specifically the tyranny of distance, add an element of difficulty that was not present in Europe. Although there were greater numbers of potential evacuees in the European Theater, access to all manners of transportation, land, sea and air, would have facilitated the evacuation of personnel. Evacuation of the Republic of Korea would be limited to air and sea only with the threat to potential Intermediate Staging Bases in Japan by the DPRKs surface to surface missile capabilities significantly hampering the bases utility in facilitating the evacuation.

The United States Ambassadors and Geographic Combatant Commanders are responsible for protection of United States citizens in their respective areas of responsibility. Accordingly, planning and practicing of procedures for Non-combatant Evacuation Operations (NEOs) are prudent and necessary especially as stability, in a Host Nation or region, waivers. This paper's initial hypothesis was that the decision to make necessary preparations for an evacuation may in fact precipitate the requirement to execute one, thus framing an undesirable decision to evacuate. As a consequence of analyzing the military assisted NEOs and drawdowns short of NEOs, the initial hypothesis was not proven but other aspects of drawdowns and NEOs were revealed which could better prepare the national security community.

Volumes have been written on the challenges and complexities of executing NEOs. This paper will not address the tactical level execution but will primarily focus on the impacts of the decision making leading up to the declaration to evacuate United States personnel. This paper will begin with an examination of the roles and responsibilities of the Department of State and Department of Defense in the planning, rehearsing, and execution of NEOs. It will then examine several NEOs executed by the United States to determine the corollaries between the steps taken prior to actual military involvement in the NEO and the final decision to execute a NEO. Additionally, this paper will analyze the actions and results of the evacuations to inform future decision makers on the consequences of actions or inactions. Finally, this paper will address recommendations for decision makers on risks for future actions or inactions leading up to a Non-combatant Evacuation Operations.

CHAPTER 2:

BACKGROUND

The current National Security Strategy clearly delineates one of the nation's enduring interests as the "the security of the United States, its citizens, and U.S. allies and partners."[1] In a period of great uncertainty on the future threats to the United States and its people and an era of tight budgets and constrained resources due to the Nation's fiscal challenges, the Defense Strategic Guidance of 2012 states "United States forces will also remain capable of conducting non-combatant evacuation operations (NEO) for American citizens overseas on an emergency basis."[2] As delineated in the *Memorandum of Agreement Between the Department of State and Defense on the Protection and Evacuation of U.S. Citizens and Nationals and Designated Other Persons From Threatened Areas:*

> In the event of an emergency abroad affecting the safety of U.S. citizens, it is the policy of the United States Government to:
> 1. Protect U.S. citizens and nationals and designated other persons, to include, when necessary and feasible, their evacuation to and welfare in relatively safe areas.
> 2. Reduce to a minimum the number of U.S. citizens and nationals and designated other persons subject to the risk of death and/or seizure as hostages.
> 3. Reduce to a minimum the number of U.S. citizens and nationals and designated other persons in probable or actual combat areas so that combat effectiveness of U.S. and allied forces is not impaired.[3]

---

[1] U.S. President, *National Security Stratgey of the United States*, (Washington DC: Government Printing Office, May 2010), 7.

[2] Department of Defense, *Sustaining U.S. Global Leadership: Priorities for 21ˢᵗ Century Defense*, (Washington DC: Department of Defense, January 2012), 6.

[3] Department of State, "Memorandum of Agreement Bewtween the Department of State and Defense on the Protection and Evacuation of U.S. Citizens and Nationals and Designated Other Persons From Threatened Areas Overseas July 1998," Department of State, http://poems.ses.state/sites/portal/seso/cms/CoMCheck/Multiple%20Content%20Type%20Library/DOS-DOD%20MOU%20on%20Evacuations.doc (accesesd March 8, 2014), 1.

The Department of State has primary authority for ensuring the safety of United States citizens abroad. Department of State responsibilities are further delineated in law by the Omnibus Diplomatic Security and Antiterrorism Act of 1986: "The Secretary of State shall develop and implement policies and programs to provide for the safe and efficient evacuation of United States Government personnel, dependents, and private United States citizens when their lives are endangered."[4] Geographic Combatant Commanders are responsible to prepare and maintain plans for the protection and evacuation for United States noncombatants.[5]

The Chief of Mission (COM) is responsible for the direction, coordination, and supervision of all United States Government executive branch employees in the country, except for personnel under the command of a United States area military commander or on the staff of an international organization.[6] The COM is also recognized in Department of Defense Directive 3025.14:

> As the President's personal representative to the host country, the (COM), or Principal Officer, is the lead federal official for the protection and evacuation of all United States noncombatants, including Department of Defense dependents.[7]

The Department of State's Emergency Planning Handbook further elaborates the COMs responsibilities:

> The COM is expected to recommend drawdown on a timely basis when circumstances warrant it. Departure may be authorized or ordered when it is of national interest to require the departure of some or all employees and their

---

[4] U.S. Congress, *Omnibus Diplomatic Security and Antiterrorism Act, U.S. Code*, vol 22, sec. 4802 (1986).

[5] U.S. Joint Chiefs of Staff. *Noncombatant Evacuation Operations*, Joint Publication 3-68 (Washington DC: Joint Chiefs of Staff, December 23, 2010), II-9.

[6] Department of State. *12 Foreign Affairs Handbook -1*. Emergency Planning Handbook . (Washington DC: Department of State, 2010), 12 FAH-1 H-121a.

[7] Department of Defense. *Evacuation of U. S. Citizens and Designated Aliens from Threatened Areas Abroad,* Department of Defense Directive 3025.14 (Washington DC: Department of Defense, February 2013), 2.

eligible family members, or if there is imminent danger to the life of the employee, the lives of the immediate family of the employee.[8]

In addition to evacuating U. S. citizens, the United States may evacuate third-country nationals (TCNs) (a TCN is an individual who is neither a citizen of the United States nor of the country in which they are employed) and host-country nationals on a case-by-case, space available, and reimbursable basis when doing so serves U.S. interests.[9]

Because two departments are involved in these complex operations, coordination is key, yet challenging. Both departments have cultural biases, vastly different planning capacities and resources. These differences in the way personnel of State and Defense perceive problems and solutions can produce better results if the differences can be managed in the pursuit of a common goal.[10] Several organizations exist to ensure coordination and cooperation between Department of State and Department of Defense. These organizations include, the Washington Liaison Group (WLG), the Regional Liaison Groups (RLG), and the Emergency Action Committee (EAC). The WLG is responsible for coordination and implementation at the national level of all emergency and evacuation plans by the Departments of State and Defense.[11] A Department of State representative chairs the WLG since they are lead federal agency for the NEOs.[12] The RLGs have been established by Department of State and Department of Defense

---

[8] Department of State. *12 Foreign Affairs Handbook -1.* Emergency Planning Handbook . (Washington DC: Department of State, 2010), 12 FAH-1 H-121c.

[9] Ibid, 12 FAH-1 Annex K 2.4 para b.1.

[10] Rosemary Hansen and LTC Rick Rife, *Defense is From Mars, State is From Venus*, (Carlisle, PA: US Army War College, May 1998), 11.

[11] Department of State. *12 Foreign Affairs Handbook -1.* Emergency Planning Handbook . (Washington DC: Department of State, 2010), 12FAH-1 H-022.4.

[12] U.S. Joint Chiefs of Staff. *Noncombatant Evacuation Operations*, Joint Publication 3-68 (Washington DC: Joint Chiefs of Staff, December 23, 2010), II-2.

collocated with combatant commands as necessary to ensure coordination of emergency and evacuation planning by the departments in the field by providing liaison between the WLG and the posts.[13] The EAC is a group of subject-matter experts from the United States Embassy or mission appointed by the COM. The EAC provides the ambassador with guidance in preparing for and responding to threats, emergencies, and other crises at the post. Tasks identified by the EAC to expedite a possible evacuation include conducting vulnerability assessments, assessing the post and host government's capabilities and limitations for emergency response, and drafting of the Emergency Action Plan (EAP) for the post and submitting it for review, approval, and publication.[14] Final approval of the EAP is required from the Department of State and it is mandated that reviews of an EAP be conducted annually.[15] Geographic Combatant Commanders are responsible for reviewing all EAPs resident in their AORs. Recommendations for adjustments due to perceived shortfalls are made through the appropriate ambassador.[16] The EAC also develops tripwires as part of the EAP and actions to take when those thresholds are met. Tripwires are conditions based criteria or circumstances that diplomatic posts use to facilitate decision making in drawdown and evacuation scenarios. These tripwires are broken down into categories based on the severity of a potential crisis. The first category includes events that indicate a growing potential for drawdown

---

[13] U.S. Joint Chiefs of Staff. *Noncombatant Evacuation Operations*, Joint Publication 3-68 (Washington DC: Joint Chiefs of Staff, December 23, 2010), II-2.

[14] Department of State. *12 Foreign Affairs Handbook -1.* Emergency Planning Handbook . (Washington DC: Department of State, 2010), 12 FAH-1 H-031a.

[15] Ibid, 12 FAH-1 H-231.

[16] U.S. Joint Chiefs of Staff. *Noncombatant Evacuation Operations*, Joint Publication 3-68 (Washington DC: Joint Cheifs of Staff, December 23, 2010), III-5.

but do not result in actual drawdown. The second and third categories of trip wires include events that could lead to authorized departure recommendations and ordered departures.

Authorized departure permits the COM some flexibility for meeting crisis situations short of ordering the departure of employees or eligible family members. Under authorized departure neither employees nor eligible family members can be compelled to leave. Ordered departure occurs when the COM or Department of State may determine that a situation has reached a point that, for their safety or other valid reasons in the national interest, eligible family members and/or certain employees should be ordered to leave post, at least temporarily. Ordered departure is not optional for the individuals under the authority of the COM.[17] The "no double standard" policy requires private U.S. citizens be given the same evacuation opportunities and assistance as U.S. government affiliated civilians. Department of State accomplishes most ordered evacuations using commercial transportation (scheduled or chartered), without the use of military personnel or assistance. However, Department of State may request a Department of Defense-assisted NEO (using Department of Defense organic or chartered transportation assets) based on the nature of the threat or the lack of availability of alternative forms of transportation.[18]

---

[17] Department of State. *12 Foreign Affairs Handbook -1.* Emergency Planning Handbook . (Washington DC: Department of State, 2010), Annex K Addendum 1.1.

[18] Department of Defense. *Evacuation of U. S. Citizens and Designated Aliens from Threatened Areas Abroad,* Department of Defense Directive 3025.14 (Washington DC: Department of Defense, February 2013), 3.

The decisions to begin drawdowns and, if necessary, to evacuate a United States embassy and the order to execute a NEO are political.[19] Downsizing the U.S. presence at an embassy is likely to be perceived by the host nation and the world that the United States lacks commitment or indicates that the United States no longer trusts the host nation to protect U.S. citizens. It is for this reason that the Department of State tends to wait as long as possible before requesting military assistance, viewing an evacuation as a failure in the diplomatic process. Addressing the sensitivity of the issue, Department of Defense Directive 3025.14 states, "diplomatic or other considerations may make the use of certain terms, such as 'noncombatant evacuation operation' (NEO), inadvisable and require the use of other terms instead."[20] The command and control structure and the political and diplomatic factors involved in timing the execution of the military support of NEOs make them different from other military operations. During NEOs, the COM, not the geographic combatant commander (GCC) or subordinate joint force commander (JFC), is the senior United States Government authority for the evacuation and, as such, is ultimately responsible for the successful completion of the NEO and the safety of the evacuees. Additionally, the uncertainty of the environment, whether permissive, uncertain or hostile, adds to the complexity of conducting NEOs. "The impact of introducing US forces into an already unstable environment could be further destabilizing."[21]

---

[19] U.S. Joint Chiefs of Staff. *Noncombatant Evacuation Operations*, Joint Publication 3-68 (Washington DC: Joint Chiefs of Staff, December 23, 2010), 10.

[20] Department of Defense. *Evacuation of U. S. Citizens and Designated Aliens from Threatened Areas Abroad,* Department of Defense Directive 3025.14 (Washington DC: Department of Defense, February 2013), 2.

[21] U.S. Joint Chiefs of Staff. *Noncombatant Evacuation Operations*, Joint Publication 3-68 (Washington DC: Joint Chiefs of Staff, December 23, 2010), I-3.

Department of Defense Directive 3025.14, *Protection and Evacuation of US Citizens and Designated Aliens in Danger Areas Abroad*, delineates the responsibility of Department of Defense to support Department of State. It assigns the responsibility to plan and conduct NEOs in support of Department of State to the GCCs. Actual evacuation assistance can be provided only upon the request by the Secretary of State (SECSTATE) to either the Secretary of Defense (SECDEF) or the President. Once requested, approved, and directed, the combatant commander (CCDR) will order assigned and/or attached forces to conduct evacuation operations in support of Department of State and the COM. Once the decision to order an evacuation has been made, the evacuation of noncombatants will generally occur in the following phases:

> 1) Standfast - When a country's political or security environment has deteriorated and it is perceived that US citizens are threatened, but an evacuation is either not required or is temporarily impossible, all US citizens are requested to "stand fast" and are given preliminary instructions for preparing to evacuate the country.
> 2) Leave Commercial - Due to the gravity of the situation, nonessential US citizens may be told to leave by commercial transportation as soon as possible.
> 3) Evacuation - When the political or security environment is believed to have deteriorated to the point that the safety of US citizens is threatened, the ambassador (with DOS approval) orders the departure of the personnel keeping only essential personnel of the country team.
> 4) Embassy or Post Closing- The situation may deteriorate to the point that the embassy must close and all remaining US citizens and embassy employees must be evacuated.[22]

If decision makers consider the levels of complexity in planning and executing a NEO, then they would understand that exercising and rehearsing this operation may be the most critical factor in the successful execution of the NEO. The Emergency Planning Handbook of the Department of State and Joint Publication 3-68 explicitly state the responsibility of both Department of State and Department of Defense to conduct

---

[22] U.S. Joint Chiefs of Staff. *Noncombatant Evacuation Operations*, Joint Publication 3-68 (Washington DC: Joint Chiefs of Staff, December 23, 2010), IV-5.

exercises of their plans. Coordination between the Department of State elements and Department of Defense elements is essential for the development of an executable military plan that supports the COM's requirements. The hurdles to successful completion of a NEO under circumstances that are described in the introduction as a worst case scenario could quickly overwhelm the plans in place if not sufficiently rehearsed or exercised. Due to the current fiscal uncertainties, it is highly probable that funding for exercises of sufficient size and scope may not be undertaken.

To better understand and evaluate the roles and responsibilities required of the Department and State and Department of Defense in planning, rehearsing, exercising and execution of evacuations it is imperative to evaluate prior examples of NEOs. Chapter three will examine the conditions that led to the beginning of a crisis that could warrant a drawdown; what necessitated the drawdown and subsequent execution of a NEO; and what can we learn from them to inform possible future scenarios?

CHAPTER 3:

SELECTED NON-COMBATANT EVACUATION OPERATIONS

Between the years of 1988 and 2007, Department of State ordered over 270

evacuations from overseas posts due to crises including civil strife, terrorist attacks,

natural disasters, conventional war threats and disease outbreaks.[1] It is evident that the

vast majority of these evacuations did not involve military assistance. In fact, in the

period from 2002 to 2007 only on four of eight-eight drawdown occasions was

Department of Defense assistance required.[2] Although military assisted NEOs are very

infrequent, it is necessary to analyze those factors that led to these NEOs in order to

determine if there is a connection between preparations and the requirement to execute.

This chapter will review several historical case studies that resulted in military assisted

NEOs in an attempt to develop this correlation.

OPERATION EAGLE PULL AND FREQUENT WIND

The U.S. combat role in Vietnam ended January 27, 1973, and the U.S. bombing

operations in Cambodia ended August 15, 1973. Initial tasking to begin planning for the

non-combatant emergency evacuation (NEMVAC) operations of Cambodia (Operation

EAGLE PULL) and Republic of Vietnam (RVN) (Operation FREQUENT WIND)

occurred in April 1973[3] and April 1974 respectively.[4]

---

[1] Government Accountability Office, *Report 08-23 State Department: Evacuation Planning and Preparations for Overseas Posts Can Be Improved,* (Washington DC: Government Accountability Office, October 2007), 1.

[2] Ibid, 10.

[3] Richard D. Johnson, *Operations Analysis Group Report No. 2-75: Summary of the Evacuation of Saigon, South Vietnam Under Operation Frequent Wind,* (San Francisco, CA May 1975), 84.

[4] Sydney H. Batchelder and D.A. Quinlan, "Operation Eagle Pull," *Marine Corps Gazette (* May 1976), 47.

Operation EAGLE PULL (OEP) planners developed four courses of action (COAs) to evacuate personnel: 1) commercial air, 2) military fixed-wing, 3) military helicopters, and 4) military fixed wing and helicopters.[5] In March 1973, Khmer Rouge forces increased their attacks around Phnom Penh concerning many that the fall of the capital was near.[6] With the assistance of U.S. airpower, Cambodian government forces counteroffensive staved off defeat. With cessation of U.S. air support because of the passage of the Cooper-Church Amendment to the Supplementary Foreign Assistance Act of 1970, it was only a matter of time before Khmer Rouge insurgent forces would gain the advantage in Cambodia.[7] By 4 April 1975, the Ambassador John Dean at Phnom Penh recommended a helicopter evacuation to on 6 April due to the country's situation on the ground. The Secretary of State directed that the fixed-wing option be utilized due to concerns of heightening the crisis with the use of a Marine Ground Security Force and helicopters. On 11 April, the Secretary of State directed the Ambassador to begin immediate evacuation using military and or civilian fixed-wing aircraft. However, the Ambassador replied that it was too late to execute a fixed wing evacuation due the possibility of the airport being in the hands of hostile forces or under heavy attack.[8]

The Amphibious Ready Group "A" and the 31st Marine Amphibious Unit had arrived off the coast of Cambodia on 4 March 1975 and would remain in the area until

---

[5] Patrick W. Urey, *U.S. Marine Corps participation in the emergency evacuations of Phnom Penh and Saigon : operations Eagle Pull and Frequent Wind*, (Washington DC: Center for Naval Analyses, 1977), xiii.

[6] Sydney H. Batchelder and D.A. Quinlan, "Operation Eagle Pull," *Marine Corps Gazette* (May 1976), 49.

[7] Ibid, 49.

[8] Patrick W. Urey, *U.S. Marine Corps participation in the emergency evacuations of Phnom Penh and Saigon : operations Eagle Pull and Frequent Wind*, (Washington DC: Center for Naval Analyses, 1977), 65.

called upon to execute the NEO. The United States Embassy confirmed that all American dependents had been evacuated by 11 March 1975.[9] Operation EAGLE PULL COA 3 (the use of military helicopters) was executed on 12 April 1975 resulting in the evacuation of 287 evacuees from Phnom Penh. The Embassy reported the number of potential evacuees on 11 April was 590. Minimal opposition was encountered and the evacuation was completed in under four and half hours.

With Congress reluctant to support further military involvement in South-East Asia, the U.S did not respond when the North Vietnamese captured South Vietnam's Phuc Long province in January 1975, a mere 80 miles from Saigon, emboldening the North Vietnamese to believe they could go further. By March 1975, North Vietnamese Army (NVA) forces had commenced their final offensive drive resulting in a deteriorating situation in DaNang and the fall of Hue before the end of the month.[10]

Planners for Operation FREQUENT WIND (OFW) developed five COAs in expectation of greater numbers of evacuees: 1) commercial air/sea lift, 2) military fixed-wing, 3) Military Sea Lift Command sea lift, 4) military helicopters and 5) military air/sea lift. Due to deteriorating conditions in South Vietnam, American citizens began departing prior to the start of OFW. By the end of March, the Department of State began drawing down personnel on a voluntary basis via commercial and charter aircraft.[11] Ordered Departure status for non-essential personnel was announced in early April.

---

[9] Patrick W. Urey, *U.S. Marine Corps participation in the emergency evacuations of Phnom Penh and Saigon : operations Eagle Pull and Frequent Wind*, (Washington DC: Center for Naval Analyses, 1977), 64.

[10] Richard D. Johnson, *Operations Analysis Group Report No. 2-75: Summary of the Evacuation of Saigon, South Vietnam Under Operation Frequent Wind*, (San Francisco, CA May 1975), 9.

[11] Ibid, 16.

Between 21-28 April, over 43,000 persons (2,600 American citizens) were evacuated by military fixed-wing aircraft from Tan Son Nhut airport in Saigon.[12] Fixed-wing aircraft was the preferred COA for executing OFW. The day the evacuation began, the Embassy was operating in a normal day-to-day alert posture.[13] However, by mid-day 29 April the airport at Saigon was under enemy fire and the evacuation by military helicopter was selected. OFW was executed on 29 and 30 April 1975, by the 9th Marine Amphibious Brigade, resulting in the evacuation of 6,968 evacuees from the Defense Attaché Office (DAO) Compound and the United States Embassy.[14]

Liberia's experience with coups began with the overthrow of the Americo-Liberian government in 1980. Americo-Liberians are descendants of freed American slaves who had dominated Liberian politics since Liberia's independence in 1847 while only comprising five percent of the population.[15] After a century and half of rule by Americo-Liberians, Samuel Doe, a native Liberian, seized power. Doe, a member of the Krahn tribe, initially was accepted as the ruler but after failing to fulfill promises his popularity began to wane and conditions were ripe for another coup. Thomas Quiwonkpa, a member of the Gios tribe, gained additional support from the former privileged Americos in exile and attempted a coup in 1985. Doe's forces defeated the

---

[12] Patrick W. Urey, *U.S. Marine Corps participation in the emergency evacuations of Phnom Penh and Saigon : operations Eagle Pull and Frequent Wind*, (Washington DC: Center for Naval Analyses, 1977), xvi.

[13] U.S. Joint Chiefs if Staff, "*Noncombatant Emergency and Evacuation (NEMVAC) Lessons Learned Survey Collection,*" United States Policy in the Vietnam War, 1969-1975, (Washington DC: Joint Chiefs of Staff, May 19, 1975), vi.

[14] Patrick W. Urey, *U.S. Marine Corps participation in the emergency evacuations of Phnom Penh and Saigon : operations Eagle Pull and Frequent Wind*, (Washington DC: Center for Naval Analyses, 1977), xv- xvi.

[15] Joseph G. Sullivan (ed), *Embassies Under Siege: Personal Accounts by Diplomats on the Front Line,* (Brassey's, United States, 1995), 134.

attempted coup and took vengeance upon the Gios tribe. This set the stage for the civil war that began in December of 1989.

The National Patriotic Front of Liberia (NPFL), led by Charles Taylor, also a member of the Gios tribe, began their insurgency to overthrow Doe. Even though widespread fighting had not yet reached Monrovia, attacks on civilians increased in the capital due to the tribal and ethnic tensions. As the civil war drew closer to Monrovia, by the end of April 1990, the embassy requested to go to an "authorized departure status." [16] Within two weeks only a few dozen essential staff remained. Due to the history of Liberia and the successful coup in 1980 and the unsuccessful coup in 1985, Embassy personnel expected that this crisis too would end relatively quickly. [17] However, this was not the case.

By May, the NFPL threatened the only international airport in Liberia, an hour away from the capital Monrovia where the United States Embassy is located, and flights ceased. [18] The members of the Armed Force of Liberia (AFL), who remained loyal to President Doe, and the NFPL engaged in bloody battles on the outskirts of Monrovia with neither gaining much ground. Reports from the Embassy caused enough alarm to have the Amphibious Ready Group (ARG), including the 22d Marine Expeditionary Unit (22 MEU), sent from Mediterranean to take up a position off the coast of Liberia by the end of May. [19] Also in late May, a third rebel group led by Prince Johnson, former lieutenant

---

[16] Joseph G. Sullivan (ed), *Embassies Under Siege: Personal Accounts by Diplomats on the Front Line,* (Brassey's, United States, 1995), 136.

[17] Ibid, 137.

[18] Ibid, 137.

[19] Andrew Petruska, *Operation Sharp Edge – The Evacuation of Liberia – A Prototype for Future Joint Littoral Operations?,* (Newport, RI: Naval War College, March 1994), 10.

to Taylor, broke away from the NFPL to form the Independent National Patriotic Front of Liberia (INPFL). The Forward Command Element, a military planning team of the 22d MEU, arrived at the embassy in late May to facilitate planning with the ships of the ARG arriving on 2 June.[20]

By early June with conditions continuing to deteriorate, the embassy went to an ordered departure via commercial means leaving only the bare minimum staff. What had once been an official community over 600 personnel was reduced to less than fifty.[21] Monrovia had been cut off by mid-July, with the NFPL and INFPL on the outskirts and Doe's AFL forces in the capital. The situation became stalemated and a decisive battle never came. As violence continued to escalate the situation deteriorated to the point that the security of the American civilians could no longer be guaranteed. Due to the absence of the United States Ambassador to Liberia, the Deputy Chief of Mission, Dennis Jett, requested military assistance. The security situation had deteriorated further to the point that American and other foreigners were actively being sought out to be presumably used as leverage to provoke United States intervention.[22] After nine weeks on station off the coast of Liberia, on 5 August 1990, the evacuation of 1,648 evacuees, which included evacuees from many nations, was completed in Liberia by the 22d MEU.[23] The 26th MEU relieved the 22d MEU in late August and continued evacuation and support operations for five and one-half more months taking out and additional 700 evacuees and

[20] Andrew Petruska, *Operation Sharp Edge – The Evacuation of Liberia – A Prototype for Future Joint Littoral Operations?,* (Newport, RI: Naval War College, March 1994), 10.

[21] Joseph G. Sullivan (ed), *Embassies Under Siege: Personal Accounts by Diplomats on the Front Line,* (Brassey's, United States, 1995), 137.

[22] Ibid, 139.

[23] Andrew Petruska, *Operation Sharp Edge – The Evacuation of Liberia – A Prototype for Future Joint Littoral Operations?,* (Newport, RI: Naval War College, March 1994), 1.

maintaining the minimal staff at the Embassy. President Doe was captured on 9 September and executed on 10 September.

OPERATION EASTERN EXIT

According to the United States Ambassador to Somalia James K. Bishop, the American civilian presence in Somalia was driven primarily by three national interests. First and most importantly, was establishing military access to ports and airfields, in particular the Berbera airfield, that had been agreed upon between United States and Somalia after the Soviet invasion of Afghanistan and the Iranian Revolution, to assist in protecting the Middle East airfields from either Soviet or Iranian threats. Secondly, it was important to keep Somalia, a predominantly Muslim nation, supportive of the coalition's efforts in defense of Saudi Arabia subsequent to the invasion of Kuwait. Finally, the humanitarian crisis stemming from the conflict between warring factions was of great concern and the United States wanted to keep the country from falling apart violently.[24]

Somalia's decent into chaos began in the late 1980s. After more than twenty years of ruthless rule by Siad Barre, resistance groups had been growing and by 1990, three main rebel organizations were operating in Somalia. These groups were the United Somali Congress (USC), Somali Patriotic Movement (SPM) and the Somali National Movement (SNM). During the summer of 1990, violence had become endemic. Rebel groups attacked embassies and government buildings. Criminal attacks, including murder, in Mogadishu against Western targets were becoming commonplace. The

---

[24] Joseph G. Sullivan (ed), *Embassies Under Siege: Personal Accounts by Diplomats on the Front Line,* (Brassey's, United States, 1995), 151.

United States Ambassador's family had even been subjected to a criminal assault at a beach resort in early September 1990.[25]

Warfare in the countryside between the resistance groups and Barre's government forces had required the withdrawal of most Americans working outside of Mogadishu. By November 1990, rebels had established positions within thirty miles of Mogadishu. As a result, due to the escalating threat of violence the Ambassador directed American staff offices relocated into the main compound and restricted travel in the capital. Signs were evident that the government was heading towards failure. In early December 1990, drawdown operations had commenced. Authorized departures were encouraged on 5 December and ordered departures were directed on 19 December, resulting in only 37 official United States personnel remaining in Mogadishu.[26]

In the midst of a bloody civil war, conditions had deteriorated to the point that the United States Ambassador requested military assistance for evacuation on 2 January 1991. On 5-6 January, 281 people from 30 different countries were evacuated from the United States Embassy in Mogadishu by elements of the Fourth Marine Expeditionary Brigade. Italy, France, Egypt, China, Germany and the Soviet Union met with varying degrees of success in evacuating their nationals.

OPERATION SILVER ANVIL

On 29 April 1992, a coup d'état occurred in Sierra Leone. The "accidental coup" was a result of the Sierra Leone Army protesting the lack of pay from the government

---

[25] Joseph G. Sullivan (ed), *Embassies Under Siege: Personal Accounts by Diplomats on the Front Line,* (Brassey's, United States, 1995), 150.

[26] Adam B. Siegel, *Eastern Exit: The Noncombatant Evacuation Operation (NEO) From Mogadishu, Somalia, in January 1991*, (Alexandria, VA: Center for Naval Analysis, 1992), 2.

which led to the President fleeing the country.[27] The National Provisional Ruling Council (NPRC), the name for the coup leaders' government, was unable to maintain total control and could not guarantee the safety of the United States Embassy and its personnel.[28] The situation nation-wide began to deteriorate quickly.[29] Looting was widespread and the Lungi Airport and Port of Freetown were closed precluding any means of commercial evacuation. By 2 May the situation in Freetown had devolved to the point that the Ambassador began preparations to position people for potential evacuation and formally requested military assisted evacuation.[30] Elements of First Battalion, Tenth Special Forces Group (Airborne) were tasked with executing the evacuation. On the morning of 3 May the embassy staff began marshalling American citizens for evacuation. An estuary separated Freetown from the airport. For this reason, it was necessary to utilize a contracted hovercraft to take evacuees from the assembly area in Freetown to the Lungi Airport for evacuation via military fixed-wing air transport. Initial estimate of evacuees from the embassy staff was only 135 people, which tripled once the evacuation began to include third country nationals. The Sierra Leonese Army (SLA) commander gave assurances to the Ambassador that his forces would not interfere with the evacuation but would not assist in the conduct either. Three days of operations, 3-5 May, resulted in the evacuation of 438 evacuees in what was termed a permissive

---

[27] William C. Fleser, *Operation Silver Anvil: Non-combatant evacuation Operation in Sierra Leone May 1992,* (Tampa, FL: USSOCOM History and Research Office, June 2001), 35.

[28] Ibid, 62.

[29] Ibid, 35.

[30] Ibid, 67.

environment but with conditions ripe for escalation. The group that conducted the coup was ousted within the year and a subsequent NEO would be executed in 1996.

OPERATION ASSURED RESPONSE

Since the NEO of 1992, Liberia remained a nation in turmoil. August 1995 brought some hope for resolution of the crisis when the six warring factions joined together to attempt to work out a solution and enacted a cease fire. The cease fire only lasted for a short time when the country returned to a state of anarchy, endangering both United States citizens and foreign nationals. United Nations Observers and the Economic Community of West African States Cease-Fire Monitoring Group (ECOMOG) were unable to maintain the cease-fire. Once again, Monrovia descended into a state of lawlessness. Fearing the inability to maintain protection of the Americans remaining in Liberia due to the expanding crisis, the United States Ambassador requested more security forces and on 7 April 1996 preparations began for a NEO.[31] Special Operations Command Europe (SOCEUR) received tasking to prepare for conducting a NEO in Liberia.[32] After successfully reinforcing the Embassy in Monrovia with a 12-man SEAL team, formal execution orders were received on 9 April to conduct a NEO. Elements of First Battalion, Tenth Special Forces Group (Airborne) provided the bulk of the ground force utilized to execute the NEO. Military helicopters evacuated personnel from the Embassy in Monrovia to the intermediate staging base at Freetown, Sierra Leone and the evacuees were subsequently flown via military fixed wing transport aircraft to the safe haven in Dakar, Senegal. The State Department assisted in arranging for follow-on

---

[31] John W. Partin, *Operation Assured Response : SOCEUR's NEO in Liberia,* (Tampa, FL: USSOCOM History and Research Office,1997), 2.

[32] Ibid, 2.

transportation of the evacuees on to their final destinations. From 10-20 April 1996 2,126 evacuees were safely extracted from Liberia.[33]

EVACUATION OF AMERICAN CITIZENS FROM LEBANON JULY 2006

On 12 July 2006, after the Hezbollah incursion of the Israeli border from Lebanon, Israel retaliated by bombing the Beirut airport and blockading the port. On 14 July, Department of State requested NEO assistance from Department of Defense. Concurrently, authorized departures began for non-emergency staff desiring to leave. The first military evacuation occurred on 16 July and Department of State announced ordered departures for non-emergency staff. The last military evacuation occurred on 2 August and Department of State terminated ordered departure status for Embassy Beirut.[34] Cyprus was the primary Intermediate Staging Base where nearly 15,000 Americans were evacuated from the war zone; it was "one of the largest overseas evacuations of American citizens in recent history."[35] One of the most cited deficiencies noted was in communication with the public. In an effort to control information and likely the perception of the severity of the problem, Department of State "initially restricted Embassy Beirut officials' ability to convey critical information via the media to Americans seeking to leave Lebanon."[36] This led to confusion on behalf of the personnel who desired to evacuate. Potential evacuees were getting unclear information on what to do and where to assemble in the early days of the crisis. Another significant aspect of the

---

[33] John W. Partin, *Operation Assured Response : SOCEUR's NEO in Liberia,* (Tampa, FL: USSOCOM History and Research Office,1997), 2.

[34] Government Accountability Office. *Report 07-893R US Evacuation From Lebanon June 2007,* (Washington DC: Government Accountability Office, June 2007), 28.

[35] Ibid, 1.

[36] Ibid, 2.

challenge and complexity of the NEO in Lebanon was that Department of Defense was asked to assist in the evacuation of non-combatants to a safe haven, as well as transport for the evacuees from Cyprus back to United States. Department of Defense normally turns over responsibility of the evacuees once out of harm's way to Department of State to assist in arranging transportation home. However, because of the large the numbers of evacuees and an already overloaded commercial airline system in Cyprus due to peak tourist season, Department of Defense assistance was required in this final step.

While all of these NEOs resulted in the use of military assistance, the steps and circumstances that led to them vary significantly. Some were conducted in war zones, some were conducted at a moment's notice, while others occurred over a large time. It is unclear why these NEOs occurred. They could have been a result of the failure of the diplomatic process. Conversely, they might have arisen when preparations for a NEO eventually precipitated the actual need for one. Further analysis follows to answer this question, which may lead to identifying lessons to inform future application. As previously discussed, NEOs vary in scale and conditions leading to execution. It is also necessary to review procedures and examples of cases that did not result in the commitment of military forces to execute a NEO. This will frame a better understanding of where and when military involvement will be necessary.

CHAPTER 4:

DRAWDOWNS

The Department of State started keeping statistics in the mid-80s regarding the number of evacuations conducted and how many of those were Department of Defense assisted. Of the over 300 evacuations that have been conducted since June 1988, fewer than 10% were assisted by the Department of Defense, and only a sub-set of those were NEOs.[1] The Office of Crisis Management Support in the Operations Center of the Department of State monitors crises worldwide, promotes contingency planning and emergency preparedness, and supports interagency evacuation planning and implementation.

> Normally, the Principal U.S. Diplomatic or Consular Representative shall request from the Department of State approval to invoke an emergency evacuation plan in an area where an emergency is expected or is developing. When hostilities or disturbances occur with complete surprise or appear imminent, the Principal U.S. Diplomatic or Consular Representative may invoke such elements of the plan as the situation warrants including requesting assistance of the appropriate military commander, while simultaneously informing the Department of State.[2]

The Department of State will always seek to use commercial or charter transport before requesting Department of Defense support. The Department's policy is to conduct evacuations by commercial means, including charters. Military-assisted

---

[1] Department of State, "Evacuations and Drawdowns", http://fsi.state.gov/fsi/lms/cmt,. (accessed March 8, 2014.)

[2] Department of State, "Memorandum of Agreement Between the Department of State and Defense on the Protection and Evacuation of U.S. Citizens and Nationals and Designated Other Persons From Threatened Area July 1998" http://poems.ses.state/sites/portal/seso/cms/CoMCheck/Multiple%20Content%20Type%20Library/DOS-DOD%20MOU%20on%20Evacuations.doc, (accessed March 8, 2014), 1.

evacuations (known as Noncombatant Evacuation Operations - NEOs) are rare and require an official request from the Department of State to the Department of Defense.

GUIDELINES FOR DRAWDOWN, DEPARTURE, AND EVACUATION

The Department of State's highest priority is protecting U.S. citizens abroad, recognizing that private U.S. citizens cannot be compelled to depart or even to follow recommendations. The following provides general guidance used by the State Department for moving to drawdown or evacuation status. Detailed guidelines and instructions are provided in their online resource *Foreign Affairs Handbook* within crisis.state.gov, which contain action checklists for the COM and members of the Emergency Action Committee (EAC).

Limiting official presence at post, which does not require Washington approval, should be considered as tensions increase or security deteriorates. Reducing numbers of incoming personnel, whether permanent employees (through annual leave or by delaying arrival dates) or by shortening temporary duty assignments can facilitate decreasing numbers without the stigma of an authorized or ordered departure. [3] It is essential that the F-77 Report of Potential Evacuees be regularly updated. It is equally important that EACs review their respective post's tripwires in which the definitions of what local events might trigger a decision to reduce staff or evacuate.

AUTHORIZED DEPARTURE AND ORDERED DEPARTURE BASICS

Departure is approved by the Under Secretary for Management in increments not to exceed 30-days with a maximum of 180 days. After 180 days, if the security

---

[3] Department of State, "Guidance on Drawdown, Evacuation or Suspension of Mission Operations," http://poems.ses.state/sites/portal/seso/cms/during/Post/Guidance%20on%20Drawdowns,%20Evacuations%20and%20Suspension%20of%20Operations.docx. (accessed March 8, 2014), 3.

situation warrants, post's operating status may become unaccompanied or partially unaccompanied.[4] The COM should communicate evacuation decision-making to the State Department in a timely way, but may act unilaterally "in extremis" when there is threat to life or limb. For authorized departures, Eligible Family Members (EFMs) and non-emergency personnel (as defined by the COM) may choose to leave post. The COM can also request authority to allow emergency personnel to travel to/from post. In ordered departures, EFMs and non-emergency personnel must leave the post; EFMs may remain at post only with Under Secretary for Management approval.[5] Authorized departure and ordered departure are flexible--they can be tailored, and even combined, to fit the embassy's particular circumstances. For example, an embassy may direct authorized departure of non-emergency personnel but ordered departure of EFMs. Authorized departure may be upgraded to ordered departure, but ordered departure cannot revert to authorized departure. Approval of authorized departure or ordered departure automatically triggers issuance of a Travel Warning, if one was not already in place.[6]

CONAKRY, GUINEA 2010

The United States Embassy in Conakry, Guinea was put under ordered departure by the Department of State on September 30, 2009 in response to growing civil unrest throughout the summer, culminating in a massacre at Conakry Football Stadium on September 28, 2009 perpetrated by members of the Presidential Guard, an elite force

---

[4] Department of State, "Guidance on Drawdown, Evacuation or Suspension of Mission Operations," http://poems.ses.state/sites/portal/seso/cms/during/Post/Guidance%20on%20Drawdowns,%20Evacuations%20and%20Suspension%20of%20Operations.docx. (accessed March 8, 2014), 2.

[5] Ibid, 6.

[6] Ibid, 6.

under the President's direct control.[7] At least 150 people were killed and over a thousand others were injured. The Presidential Guard also publicly raped many of the female protestors. Forty-eight hours later, the diplomatic post was ordered by Washington to request authorized departure status, later becoming ordered departure, and by week's end had evacuated all non-essential staff and family members.[8]

Due to the events in Conakry beginning on September 28, the diplomatic post underwent virtually no pre-drawdown activities. Though the Embassy was closed beginning on September 29 to all but essential staff due to the civil unrest, a subsequent review of established diplomatic post tripwires showed that most tripwires had not been crossed. Nevertheless, the diplomatic post was directed the next day on September 30 to send a request for authorized departure. The request was answered with a directive for ordered departure, as all non-essential staff and families had no choice as to whether they could stay or leave. The decision for ordered departure was not based on reporting from the field as the tripwires had not been crossed. While it is understandable that most evacuations will never go according to plans as outlined in an EAP, ignoring the document entirely in times of crisis negates its purpose and is a disservice to the amount of time post employees dedicate to its publication.[9]

First, the sudden directive from Washington precluded any pre-drawdown preparations, putting the diplomatic post at a significant disadvantage on many fronts.

---

[7] Department of State, "Lessons Learned from AMEMB Conakry's Ordered Departure", http://poems.ses.state/sites/portal/seso/cms/after/Lessons/2010%20Conakry%20173%20-%20Lessons%20Learned,%20Ordered%20Departure.doc, (accessed March 8, 2014), 1.

[8] Ibid, 1.

[9] Ibid, 2.

The embassy was unable to conduct pre-drawdown activities such as administrative issues surrounding the evacuation (i.e., town hall meetings, distribution of evacuation packets, communicating evacuation plan, and other pertinent evacuation information.) Conakry, however, had a 72 hour period to begin, organize, and execute an evacuation. Insufficient warning was difficult at both Conakry and supporting adjacent embassies, Dakar and Freetown, who had in many cases even greater administrative hurdles to overcome in receiving evacuees for long term stays.[10]

Challenges occurred when the post reported a stabilizing situation in country while Washington authorities openly advised caution towards lifting ordered departure. What occurred next were disagreements, discrepancies in reporting, and often misunderstandings of the situation leading to Washington failing to acknowledge a stabilizing and markedly improving political and security climate.[11] Lack of clear communications within one's own department can have significant influence on operations.

This evacuation also led to the requirement for expanded Crisis Management Exercises (CME) to effectively rehearse people's responsibilities during times of crisis. Ordered departure by its very nature will always be a process that marks employees and evacuees with an acute sense of loss.[12]

---

[10] Department of State, "Lessons Learned from AMEMB Conakry's Ordered Departure", http://poems.ses.state/sites/portal/seso/cms/after/Lessons/2010%20Conakry%20173%20-%20Lessons%20Learned,%20Ordered%20Departure.doc, (accessed March 8, 2014), 4.

[11] Ibid, 3.

[12] Department of State, "Lessons Learned from AMEMB Conakry's Ordered Departure", http://poems.ses.state/sites/portal/seso/cms/after/Lessons/2010%20Conakry%20173%20-%20Lessons%20Learned,%20Ordered%20Departure.doc, (accessed March 8, 2014), 4.

The primary lesson learned from this drawdown was Emergency Action Plans (EAP) must be followed.[13] Not only were the tripwires in Conakry's EAP not adhered to, but a publication of Conakry's reverse tripwires to end ordered departure had little effect. Additionally, in the future, reverse tripwires should in fact be a reverse image of the very tripwires that triggered ordered departure to begin with, rather than a new set of conditions written in the context of the existing security situation. Not adhering to the EAP and disregarding of tripwires increased the uncertainty and difficulty in executing the drawdown. Embassy Conakry reported that with ordered departure it is evident that the most important part of evacuation is not the evacuation itself, but the pre-drawdown activities where the evacuation is organized and communicated. After all was said and done, however, Embassy Conakry demonstrated it could effectively evacuate in less than 72 hours.

ARAB SPRING 2011

The events of the Arab Spring in early 2011 led to unanticipated evacuations of Embassies Cairo and Tunis and the suspension of operations at Embassy Tripoli.[14] Communications failure was identified as the biggest vulnerability during the rapid development of crises in Cairo, Tunis, and Tripoli. In Cairo, cellular networks, satellite phones and other means of communication either failed or were shut down by the host government, and Tripoli and Tunis had only intermittent telecom capabilities. Some embassy residences did not have landline telephones making communications to and from them difficult or impossible. These failures occurred during times of significant

---

[13] Department of State, "Lessons Learned from AMEMB Conakry's Ordered Departure", http://poems.ses.state/sites/portal/seso/cms/after/Lessons/2010%20Conakry%20173%20-%20Lessons%20Learned,%20Ordered%20Departure.doc, (accessed March 8, 2014), 7.

[14] Ibid, 3.

unrest when families were restricted to safe havens for several days with minimal communication options. As a practical consequence, country team members off compound were essentially cut off from the embassy.

Diplomatic posts should regularly test all means of communication and ensure backup power supplies are available both on-site and alternate locations. Cairo and Tripoli highlighted investment in mobile communication packages that operate independently from local infrastructure as key to their ability to function when other means of communication collapsed.[15] Cairo also relied on radios to communicate, highlighting the importance of regular radio tests and of insuring that all family members know how to operate their radio in the event that the employee cannot return to his or her residence due to disruptions in the city or embassy staffing needs. Tunis stressed having up-to-date contact lists at all locations, as well as established procedures to account for the entire community, including locally employed staff (LES).[16]

Communication with the private U.S. citizen community was also challenging. With internet and cell networks down, Cairo relied on radio broadcasts, newspaper announcements, and notices at tourist hotels to disseminate information about the security situation and evacuations to the general public.[17] In today's social media literate world, diplomatic posts should explore the expanded use of social media for public diplomacy and consular response, while remaining mindful that these platforms may encourage public discussion of sensitive or protected information. The bottom line however, is that

---

[15] Department of State, "Evacuation Lessons Learned From Arab Spring Posts," http://poems.ses.state/sites/portal/seso/cms/after/Lessons/2011%20State%20121343%20-%20Lessons%20Learned%20from%20Arab%20Spring%20Posts.doc, (accessed March 8, 2014) , 1.

[16] Ibid, 2.

[17] Ibid, 3.

diplomatic posts must proactively establish an effective plan for communicating with private U.S. citizens during a crisis, rather than waiting until a crisis occurs.

Recent evacuations also illustrated how rapidly a challenging situation can become even more complex if evacuation planning has been focused on a single airport or seaport.[18] Diplomatic posts must explore and plan for more than one evacuation method, including land, air, and sea options, with particular attention to military facilities that may remain under government control with better security during civil unrest. In Cairo, security conditions made road travel dangerous and conditions at the airport chaotic. In Tripoli, a complex security situation and lack of clarity regarding flight clearances made the seaport the better evacuation option.[19] Where possible, diplomatic posts should seek advance blanket diplomatic landing clearances at air and seaports for use in evacuations. Diplomatic posts should also proactively contact nearby diplomatic posts that might receive evacuees to obtain information regarding entry requirements into those countries for private U.S. citizens, diplomatic passport holders, and U.S. government chartered transport.

Dependence on heavily traveled or limited internal transportation routes can also impede crisis response. In Cairo, many primary roadways were impassable because of informal checkpoints staffed by unidentified armed groups.[20] In addition, if road travel becomes difficult or dangerous, some mission personnel may be cut off from the chancery. Diplomatic posts should drill the Embassy community to ensure all personnel

---

[18] Department of State, "Evacuation Lessons Learned From Arab Spring Posts," http://poems.ses.state/sites/portal/seso/cms/after/Lessons/2011%20State%20121343%20-%20Lessons%20Learned%20from%20Arab%20Spring%20Posts.doc, (accessed March 8, 2014) , 3.

[19] Ibid, 4.

[20] Ibid, 5.

and family members are familiar with alternate routes to various locations. However, posts should also have a plan to assist personnel or EFMs who are unable to reach a central location. Diplomatic posts should identify additional safe haven options in Emergency Action Plans (EAP), including residential compounds, in the event personnel or EFMs must shelter in place during prolonged unrest.[21]

Disruption to host government and local services are a significant obstacle in all crisis scenarios. Whether a natural disaster overwhelms the host government's capacity to respond, or a sudden change in government where key decision-makers are no longer able to assist, a host government collapse or severe disruption can dramatically change the response equation. A breakdown in host nation security services is most likely to expose EAP vulnerabilities.[22] In Cairo, the loss of key host government contacts, while problematic, highlighted the important role LES can play in responding to a crisis.[23] During a crisis, it is likely that many of the embassy's host nation government contacts can become unreachable, LES communicated with working-level contacts including airport expediters for practical information and assistance. A Tripoli expediter obtained fresh food for passengers on the evacuation ferry when its departure was delayed several days because of weather; absent those provisions, departing U.S. citizens would have faced an even more challenging situation.[24]

Well-developed tripwires facilitate evacuation decisions and must be communicated and understood with the Department of State early in a crisis. Both Cairo

---

[21] Department of State, "Evacuation Lessons Learned From Arab Spring Posts," http://poems.ses.state/sites/portal/seso/cms/after/Lessons/2011%20State%20121343%20-%20Lessons%20Learned%20from%20Arab%20Spring%20Posts.doc, (accessed March 8, 2014) , 5.

[22] Ibid, 5.

[23] Ibid, 6.

[24] Ibid, 8.

and Tripoli crossed established tripwires very quickly but regularly revisited them as the crisis developed, adjusting tripwires to keep pace with events on the ground. Reverse tripwires, conditions or criteria that assist decision makers, will help to determine when the diplomatic post should request that Washington lift evacuation status. When developed early, reverse tripwires that establish the conditions for returning to normal operations can help frame the situation for both the diplomatic post and the Department of State.

Another consideration to support the drawing down of posts is the consideration of requesting temporary duty (TDY) personnel support. Early in its crisis, Embassy Cairo requested TDY support for its evacuation planning. Consular Affairs TDY support personnel brought consular materials directly to airport rally points , as well as items for evacuees.[25] TDY assistance from the Bureau of Public Affairs handled media requests. Supplemental support from the Bureau of Diplomatic Security similarly enhanced security for mission personnel. Washington must be notified as soon as possible if a request for Department of Defense assistance is being considered.

If a Task Force (TF) is set up in Washington, it becomes the Embassy's primary interlocutor within the Department. During recent evacuations, TFs enabled posts to conserve resources by taking on, or at a minimum assisting with, necessary logistical and administrative tasks, such as outreach and notifications to American citizens.[26] The TF can assist with clearing and posting emergency and travel messages for U.S. citizens, expediting approval for alternate safe haven or other requests, and coordinating TDY

---

[25] Department of State, "Evacuation Lessons Learned From Arab Spring Posts," http://poems.ses.state/sites/portal/seso/cms/after/Lessons/2011%20State%20121343%20-%20Lessons%20Learned%20from%20Arab%20Spring%20Posts.doc, (accessed March 8, 2014) , 8.

[26] Ibid , 7.

assistance. The TF will also track requests for interagency support, including military teams, and will disseminate situation reports.

The events of the Arab Spring highlighted the necessity for crisis planning exercises and drills as they were deemed to be keys to the success of the evacuations.[27] Diplomatic posts that test procedures and equipment regularly are best positioned for a crisis. If a diplomatic post identifies vulnerabilities during these tests, it should reach out to the Department of State to discuss specific needs. Also, they need to keep classified holdings at a manageable level and regularly conduct communication, relocation, and destruction drills. Although each diplomatic post and crisis is unique, training for all imaginable scenarios will provide a solid basis for action during even the most unexpected situations.

Having examined the Department of State process and cases of drawdowns not involving military assisted evacuations, it is now necessary to analyze whether or not evacuation actions taken during crises in a host nation can lead to exacerbation of the crises that subsequently leads to a request for Department of Defense assistance to conduct a Noncombatant Evacuation Operation. Chapter five will discuss what lessons or recommendations can be made to facilitate greater coordination between the Department of State and Defense in order to meet the increasing challenges of a complex, uncertain future security environment as well as a fiscally constrained United States Government?

---

[27] Department of State, "Evacuation Lessons Learned From Arab Spring Posts," http://poems.ses.state/sites/portal/seso/cms/after/Lessons/2011%20State%20121343%20-%20Lessons%20Learned%20from%20Arab%20Spring%20Posts.doc, (accessed March 8, 2014) , 8.

CHAPTER 5:

ANALYSIS

The decision of the COM to evacuate American citizens from a host nation communicates to the host nation government and the world a clear message that the United States has lost confidence in the host nation's ability to protect American citizens. Since it is the goal of the Department of State to remain engaged and promote United States' national interests abroad, even the preparations preceding a NEO, including authorized or ordered drawdowns of United States personnel, may have serious diplomatic and political ramifications. The perceived lack of confidence in the host nation government may also signal other nations, international agencies, or competing factions within the host nation to react in such a manner as to heighten or accelerate the crisis. These actions (drawdowns) or evacuations of a diplomatic post may reduce the ability of the COM to potentially avert the crisis. It is for these reasons that Department of State is not inclined to conduct a NEO and appears to postpone drawdown and evacuation decisions as long as possible thus increasing risk to a successful outcome of a NEO.

Evidence indicates that only a small number of embassy drawdowns result in the requirement for military assistance. There have been over 300 evacuations from overseas posts ordered by Department of State since 1988. Although seven military assisted NEOs are examined in this paper, the vast majority of evacuations are conducted without the assistance of military personnel and equipment. Is this the result of adept diplomacy or is it the result of a mindset to use the military only as a last resort? Why didn't more of these evacuations lead to requests for military assistance?

As was seen in all the instances of military assisted NEOs reviewed in this paper, the ambassador and the commanders will have their actions and decisions monitored or even controlled from the highest levels of the United States Government. Decisions affecting the conduct of NEOs such as dictating when to execute a NEO, method of executing the NEO (i.e., fixed wing vs. rotary wing vs. surface or a combination of transportation methods), and establishment of Rules of Engagement for example, are all made at the highest policy levels. It is evident that due to potentially significant and irreversible diplomatic repercussions of an embassy drawdown or NEO, the decision to begin to implement drawdown procedures or announce an evacuation must be made with extreme caution. In the case of the Conakry ordered departure, Washington dictated the evacuation.

In an effort to minimize the potential negative diplomatic outcomes, the Department of State will make every effort to conduct the drawdown as quietly as possible. The perception of U.S. inability to support the host nation government or lack of commitment to the host nation government could lead to greater loss of influence in the region amongst partner nations and adversaries. One example of the United States' desire to minimize potential negative diplomatic consequences by quietly removing non-essential personnel is evident by the drawdown of 400 American citizens from West Africa in 2004 solely with the assistance of foreign government arranged aircraft.[1]

Communication and coordination between the embassy staff and the military forces tasked with executing a military assisted evacuation are paramount to the successful completion of a NEO. Joint doctrine has evolved over the past couple of

---

[1] Government Accountability Office, *Report 08-23 State Department: Evacuation Planning and Preparations for Overseas Posts Can Be Improved,* (Washington DC: Government Accountability Office, October 2007), 15.

decades that has emphasized the necessity for this mutual understanding of objectives and chains of command. Unity of effort, a tenant of all military planning and execution, while difficult to achieve when dealing with multiple governmental departments due to organizational cultural differences, is of utmost importance in conducting NEOs and is simplified by the ambassador's authority over actions of all United States Government agencies in the country.

The Government Accounting Office in an October 2007 report, *Evacuation Plans and Preparations for Overseas Posts Can Be Improved*, identified several recommendations for Department of State to better conduct NEOs. These recommendations included: 1) designation of a single entity to ensure that EAPs are prepared and reviewed annually, 2) ensuring diplomatic posts generate standardized after action reports with lessons learned and a mechanism for sharing and utilizing them while training post staffs, 3) refining F-77 reports (report generated by embassies of United States personnel being tracked for evacuation purposes) to be of greater value in planning for NEOs, 4) improving training for EAC members and 5) strengthening the department's ability to rehearse post emergency procedures.

NEOs can be directed without warning because of sudden drastic changes in a country's government such as a coup, a sudden hostile threat to United States citizens from a force within or external to a host country such as in the case of an impending war.[2] It is for these reasons that preparedness is such an essential component of readiness. However, according to a 2007 GAO report, "while all posts are required to review and update their EAPs once a year, we [GAO] found almost 40 percent of posts

---

[2] Ray L. Clark Jr, *Noncombatant evacuation operations : major considerations for the operational commander,* (Newport, RI: Naval War College, June 1995), 3-4.

surveyed had not updated their EAP in 18 months or longer."[3] Despite the perception that diplomacy has failed in the event of a NEO being executed, it is incumbent upon the leadership and personnel involved to ensure that all matters that are in their control (contingency planning and preparations) are adequately completed and refined/reviewed on a timely basis.

In an effort to draw correlations between the case studies, a comparison of the timing of the decision to begin drawdowns, the speed of the escalation of the crisis and the nature of the conflict will be examined. In the case of Operation EAGLE PULL and Operation FREQUENT WIND, indications of the requirement for an evacuation were clear enough that planning orders went out over one year before the actual evacuation took place. Ordered Departure status for non-essential personnel in Cambodia was given on 11 March and the NEO was conducted just 30 days later. The timeline from ordered departure status to conduct of the NEO was even shorter in Saigon, where non-essential personnel were ordered to depart in early April and the NEO was executed less than 30 days later.

The amphibious force arrived off the coast of Liberia in preparation for execution of Operation SHARP EDGE in August 1990. The final decision to execute a military assisted NEO could be considered a fait accompli? It can be argued that once the first helicopter touched down President Doe lost his legitimacy.[4] With the loss of his legitimacy, it was only a matter of time before a military assisted NEO would be

---

[3] Government Accountability Office, *Report 08-23 State Department: Evacuation Planning and Preparations for Overseas Posts Can Be Improved,* (Washington DC: Government Accountability Office, October 2007), 5.

[4] S.L. Bumgardner, "A NEO is More Than A Maneuver,*"* Small Wars Journal.com. http://www.Smallwarsjournal.com/documents/bumgardner.pdf (accessed 12 September 2013), 9.

necessary. It took only four months from the arrival of the FCE at the Embassy in May for the Embassy to be evacuated and President Doe captured and executed. Authorized departure status was announced in late April and ordered departure status was announced in early June.

In the case of Operation EASTERN EXIT, the deterioration of the situation in Somalia transpired very rapidly. Authorized departure status was announced on 5 December and ordered departure status was announced on 19 December. The final step, a military assisted NEO, was conducted just over 30 days after authorized departures were announced.

In the case of Operation SILVER ANVIL, the NEO of Sierra Leone in 1992, the situation devolved so quickly that the time from the crisis, caused by the the 29 April coup, to the request for military assistance of 2 May and evacuation 3-5 May took place in just over a week. Arguably, the diminished United States Government presence in Sierra Leone after SILVER ANVIL contributed to the conditions that led to a subsequent NEO. These conditions festered due to the decrease in United States influence in Sierra Leone therefore contributing to subsequent internal strife and another NEO conducted in 1996.

The crises in Liberia in 1996 and Lebanon in 2006, both deteriorated so rapidly that military assisted NEOs began within less than a week of the crisis. By 7 April 1996, the Ambassador in Liberia requested a NEO which ended up being executed 10-20 April. The crisis in Lebanon began on 12 July, authorized departure status was announced on 14 July, the first military assisted evacuation took place on 16 July, the same day ordered departure status was announced.

The natures of conflicts that could lead to the requirement to conduct a NEO are varied and unpredictable. Operation FREQUENT WIND and Operation EAGLE PULL were NEOs conducted in nations that United States had conducted and supported combat operations within the past two years. Operations SHARP EDGE, EASTERN EXIT, SILVER ANVIL and ASSURED RESPONSE occurred in nations where internal domestic political turmoil, whether civil war or coup, led to the necessity to evacuate United States personnel. The evacuation of Lebanon in 2006 was the result of a conflict between a nation, Israel, and a terrorist organization, Hezbollah in Lebanon, that endangered the lives of United States citizens in the region.

Many developing nations are currently troubled by growing populations with insufficient infrastructures, a widening economic gap and other destabilizing conditions. These conditions will require NEOs to remain an operational requirement for the foreseeable future. According to the *Failed State Index of 2010*, " the top 10 slots (of the Failed State Index) have rotated among just 15 unhappy countries...state failure, it seems, is a chronic condition."[5] It is therefore imperative that Department of Defense and Department of State continue to improve and refine doctrine as well as place the needed emphasis upon its importance. The Memorandum of Understanding between Department of State and Department of Defense and their respective doctrines for executing NEOs have arguably supported the successful completion of NEOs over the years. Perhaps, in the current and expected future reduced fiscal environment, maybe it's time to develop cross department doctrine that will further enhance the symbiotic relationship of Department of State and Department of Defense in the conduct of NEOs. The significant

---

[5] Foreign Policy and Fund for Peace, "The Failed States Index", *Foreign Policy* (July-August 2010), 76.

disparity in the number of drawdowns and actual number of military assisted NEOs highlights the care with which the United States Government and the Department of State make the decision to execute drawdowns and NEOs.

The departure status is not a trigger for engaging a Department of Defense assisted NEO, and there is no requirement to follow a progression. If a situation erupts, State may jump straight to ordered departure or even a temporary suspension of operations. State may request military assistance for a NEO from the Department of Defense, as only a last resort, once options involving scheduled commercial and chartered commercial transportation are no longer viable. From State's perspective, departure status and the method of evacuation support are two separate decisions based on the same set of circumstances.[6]

The future scenario that was proposed at the beginning of this paper would challenge our nation's ability to respond to the crisis. Tens of thousands of evacuees on a densely populated Korean peninsula and Intermediate Staging Bases that are vulnerable to DPRKs ballistic missile inventory are only a couple of the specific challenges. Alexander Downes, in his book *Targeting Civilians in War*, argues that civilian victimization is more likely to occur in "wars of attrition – conflicts characterized by static, positional warfare, sieges, or counterinsurgency – and wars in which a belligerent intended to conquer and annex its neighbors land."[7] In the DPRKs decision calculus, Kim Jung Un could be more concerned with allowing United States non-combatants to leave prior to conducting any attack than the threat of or actual launching of attacks

---

[6] Interview with State Department SME by author, March 17, 2014.

[7] Alexander B. Downes, *Targeting Civilians in War*, (Ithaca, NY: Cornell University Press, 2008), 244.

without the United States non-combatants in a position to be threatened. An announced authorized departure of United States non-combatants could accelerate the DPRKs decision making process to attack. Due to the significant consequences that could result from a decision to drawdown United States non-combatants from ROK, it is evident that those decisions are held at the highest levels of government due to their political nature.

One recommendation to facilitate greater cooperation and coordination between departments for the planning of evacuations is to establish a mutually agreed upon tiered system. Possible tiers for consideration could be: 1) Foreseeable (Saigon), 2) Eminent (Mogadishu), and 3) Unexpected (Freetown). Given limited resources, this tiered system suggests that planners could more efficiently direct advance NEO planning groups to areas identified for likely future NEOs, followed by countries that have high levels of chronic instability that may trigger a NEO, followed by a capacity to rapidly respond to unexpected threats that may erupt and require a NEO.

Joint training is valuable; however, the State Department does not have the resources to participate in all of the training requests they receive from the Department of Defense and its components.[8] Another recommendation to improve coordination is to institute a more strategic, centralized approach to training and joint planning on the basics of NEOs. This would ensure a better understanding by each department of each other's capabilities and limitations. This in turn would support the Geographic Commands work with consular sections at diplomatic posts on country-specific issues and reviewing of plans that would in-turn generate greater efficiency and effectiveness. Additionally, there are some fundamental differences in the way that the Department of State and the

---

[8] Interview with State Department SME by author, March 17, 2014.

Department of Defense are individually accustomed to developing plans and problem solving which, if addressed, would significantly improve coordination and cooperation efforts.

The greatest challenge in the interaction of Department of State and Department of Defense with respect to NEO planning, supporting and execution is ensuring that Department of State and Department of Defense have a fundamental understanding about each other's organizations before sitting down to coordinate for planning as both departments generally do not interpret things to have the same meaning. Further, State is accustomed to functioning with a dearth of resources, so requirement discussions are consumed by re-learning each departments capabilities and limitations. David Kay, who briefly worked with Jay Garner prior to Operation Iraqi Freedom stated, "there is a real lack of planning capacity at the Department of State."[9] The fundamental breakdowns in communications between the departments lie in that: 1) by law, private U.S. citizens are under no obligation to tell Department of State where they are and are not required to leave a crisis location, the F-77 report is a best estimate; and 2) State isn't accustomed to having resources at their disposal, they have a very difficult time getting into a mind-set of providing requirements.[10]

There are numerous regulatory documents that outline the roles and responsibilities of both departments in support of evacuation operations abroad. However, that due to the security environment and the fiscal constraints that our nation finds itself today and in the future, a mutually signed, regulatory document that carries more weight than Memorandum of Agreement is necessary. This document could align a

---

[9] Michael R Gordon and General Bernard E. Trainor, *Cobra II*, (New York: Vintage, 2006), 159.

[10] Interview with State Department SME by author, March 17, 2014.

more strategic way to enhance communication and cooperation by establishing

centralized fundamental training on each other's agencies, policies, and procedures. The

necessity to work together to understand each departments unique characteristics is

highlighted in *Defense is From Mars, State is From Venus*:

> Today's challenges, however, are creating new demands on both agencies. To satisfy the increased demands requires each agency to develop an understanding and appreciation for the other that includes their respective approaches to problem solving, capabilities and limitations, organizational structure, training programs and the external considerations that impact on each.[11]

Continued efforts to close the gap on the understanding of NEOs between Department of

State and Department of Defense could be addressed in this document. NEO

coordination and cooperation are critical and any steps that can be made to enhance the

ability to work together need to be pursued. If the Departments had better understanding

of how the other works, they would be able to work together more effectively.[12]

The amount of emphasis the Department of State places on the decision to begin

drawdown of posts clearly indicates that it assumes that any pre-emptive actions can have

an negative or deleterious impact on the diplomatic situation in the host nation or the

region. What is essential is that the Department of State and Department of Defense

continue to highlight the importance of interagency cooperation in the conduct NEOs.

Both departments have come a long way in the past few decades with regards to

cooperation and understanding of the capabilities and limitations of the other when faced

with conducting a NEO. It is the responsibility of the planners of both departments to

---

[11] Rosemary Hansen and LTC Rick Rife, *Defense is From Mars, State is From Venus*, (Carlisle, PA: US Army War College, May 1998), 2.

[12] Interview with State Department SME by author, March 17, 2014.

continue to mature this cooperation in order to prevent a crisis from overwhelming the Nation's ability to react and protect its citizens in a foreign country.

CHAPTER 6:

CONCLUSION

The objective of this paper was to review the circumstances and timing of the execution of several NEOs and several evacuations that did not result in the use of military assistance with the supposition that necessary preparatory actions to NEOs in fact further deteriorated the stability of the crisis thus mandating a NEO. These cases were then analyzed to determine if the decision to make necessary preparations, actions including authorized and ordered departures, may in fact precipitate the requirement to execute a NEO. Based on the number of evacuations that have been conducted since 1988, it can be concluded that the initial supposition is not valid and the decision to begin a drawdown does not necessitate the need to conduct a military assisted NEO. Another conclusion is that the Department of State will attempt to take all steps and actions necessary to keep United States citizens safe while also taking into consideration the significant diplomatic and political statement that is being made when an Embassy or diplomatic post either minimizes staff or evacuates all personnel based on threats. Delaying the decision as long as possible in the desire to avoid the appearance of lack of confidence in the host nation often results in a more complicated evacuation. The action of delaying the decisions to begin a drawdown or evacuation shows the world and the host nation that the United States has confidence in the host nation's ability to ensure the safety of American citizens.

It is therefore incumbent upon the Department of State and Department of Defense to ensure training and expanded cooperation is not a casualty of decreased budgets. The ability of Department of State and Department of Defense to successfully protect United States citizens abroad is a shared responsibility. The vast majority of drawdowns are accomplished as quietly as possible. However, failure to ensure the safety of United States personnel overseas has negative ramifications on American credibility. The attack on the Consular Office in Benghazi, Libya in 2012 and the death of the United States Ambassador and three other Americans has set the path for what has been commonly referred to as the "new normal." This crisis deteriorated even in the absence of preparations for a drawdown, highlighting the unpredictable nature of conflict in the world today. In response, the Department of Defense has positioned additional assets within the U. S. European Command area of operations in order to better respond to potential threats in Africa. This capability was recently utilized for the military assisted drawdown of embassy personnel in South Sudan due to significant instability in the world's newest nation. Forecasting where the next requirement for a drawdown will occur is beyond the abilities of the United States Government. What can be accomplished is a continued appreciation for the troubled spots around the globe and the continued refinement of the relationship between the Departments of State and Defense.

NEOs will continue to be a requirement in the ever changing and challenging geo-political environment the United States finds itself. The dynamics of the decisions to conduct preparatory actions or to begin evacuation operations will have significant impact on the timing, access, and potential environments encountered by relief forces. For these reasons the Department of Defense and Department of State need to continue to push for greater interagency cooperation and coordination. A framework for NEO planning and Joint Doctrine capitalizing on the unique competencies of each organization are potential solutions to greater cooperation and coordination to ensure that both

Departments continue to successfully execute evacuations. Increased emphasis on training and education of State Department and Defense Department personnel who plan and execute drawdowns are essential. The commitment of both departments to achieve greater cohesion will showcase a whole-of-government approach to these potential operations. Past success in NEOs does not ensure future success, especially in a more dynamic and multipolar world. Department of State and Department of Defense leaders must recognize that only by capitalizing on each others unique competencies will they be able to navigate the increasingly challenging and perplexing security environment of the future.

"The Joint Operating Environment 2010 envisions a future characterized by complexity, uncertainty and rapid change."[1] The *Quadrennial Defense Review 2014* highlights one of the Joint Force responsibilities is "…responding to crises to executing non-combatant evacuations…"[2] It also highlights that unless congressional action prevents sequestration in FY 2016, the Department of Defense will incur increased levels of risk for some missions. The Department will "continue to experience gaps in training and maintenance over the near term and will have a reduced margin of error in dealing with risks of uncertainty in a dynamic and shifting security environment over the long term."[3]

The successful completion of over 300 evacuations, ranging from authorized departures to military assisted evacuations and NEOs since 1988 does not preclude both

---

[1] U.S. Office of the Chairman of the Joint Chiefs of Staff, *Joint Operational Access Concept*, (Washington DC: Office of the Chairman of the Joint Chiefs of Staff 17, Jan 2012), 9.

[2] Office of the Secretary of Defense, *Quadrennial Defense Review 2014*, (Washington DC: Department of Defense, March 2014), 22.

[3] Office of the Secretary of Defense, *Quadrennial Defense Review 2014*, (Washington DC: Department of Defense, March 2014), IV.

the Department of State and Department of Defense from working towards greater

efficiency and effectiveness. In the context of today's challenges, this paper puts forth

recommendations to achieve greater cooperation and coordination.

BIBLIOGRAPHY

Batchelder, Sydney H., and Quinlan, D. A. *"Operation Eagle Pull."* *Marine Corps Gazette* (May 1976): 46-50.

Blanchard, Christopher E. "Noncombatant Evacuation Operations." *Marine Corps Gazette* (March 1997): 56-62.

Bumgardner, S.L. *"A NEO is More Than A Maneuver"*. Small Wars Journal.com. http://www.Smallwarsjournal.com/documents/bumgardner.pdf (accessed 12 September 2013).

Clark, Ray L. *Noncombatant evacuation operations : major considerations for the operational commander.* Newport, RI: Naval War College, 1995.

Davis, Mark A. *Joint Considerations for Planning and Conducting Noncombatant Evacuation Operations.* Newport, RI: Naval War College, 2007.

de Marcellus, Paul C. *Interoperability Issues in Noncombatant Evacuation Operations.* Newport, RI: Naval War College, 2008.

Downes, Alexander B. *Targeting Civilians in War.* Ithaca, NY: Cornell University Press, 2008.

Fleser, William C. *Operation Silver Anvil: Non-combatant evacuation Operation in Sierra Leone May 1992.* Tampa, FL: USSOCOM History and Research Office, June 2001.

Gordon, Michael R. and General Trainor, Bernard E. *Cobra II.* New York: Vintage, 2006.

Hansen, Rosemary and Rife, Rick. *Defense is From Mars, State is From Venus.* Carlisle, PA: US Army War College, May 1998.

Johnston, Richard D. *Operations Analysis Group Report No. 2-75: Summary of the Evacuation of Saigon, South Vietnam Under Operation Frequent Wind.* San Francisco, CA, May 1975.

Lambert, Kirk S. *Noncombatant Evacuation Operations - Plan now or pay later.* Newport, RI: Naval War College, June 1992.

Office of the Secretary of Defense. *Quadrennial Defense Review 2014.* Washington DC: Department of Defense, March 2014.

Omnibus Diplomatic Security and Antiterrorism Act. U.S. Code. Vol. 22, sec. 4802 (1986).

Partin, John W. *Operation Assured Response : SOCEUR's NEO in Liberia.* Tampa, FL: USSOCOM History and Research Office, 1997.

Petruska, Andrew. *Operation Sharp Edge – The Evacuation of Liberia – A Prototype for Future Joint Littoral Operations?* Newport, RI: Naval War College, March 1994.

Siegel, Adam B. *Eastern Exit: The Noncombatant Evacuation Operation (NEO) From Mogadishu, Somalia, in January 1991.* Alexandria, VA: Center for Naval Analysis, 1992.

————. *Non-combatant Evacuation Operations: An Analysts How- To Guide.* Alexandria, VA: Center For Naval Analyses, August 1993.

Stahl, David T. *Noncombatant evacuation operations in support of the national military strategy : a monograph.* Ft Leavenworth, MO: School of Advanced Military Studies, United States Army Command and General Staff College, 1992.

Standifer, Kate M. *Working Together during Noncombatant Evacuation Operations.* Newport, RI: Naval War College, 2008.

Sullivan, Joseph G (ed). *Embassies Under Siege: Personal Accounts by Diplomats on the Front Line.* Brassey's, US, 1995.

"The Failed States Index 2010." *Foreign Policy,* (July-August 2010): 76-79.

Treutler, Christian H. *Department of Defense Noncombatant Evacuation Operations in the Federal Republic of Germany: Time for Tough Decisions.* Maxwell AFB, AL: Air War College, May 1989.

U.S. Department of Defense. *Sustaining U.S. Global Leadership: Priorities for 21st Century Defense.* Washington DC: Department of Defense, January 2012.

————. *Evacuation of U. S. Citizens and Designated Aliens from Threatened Areas Abroad.* Department of Directive 3025.14. Washington DC: Department of Defense, February 2013.

U.S. Department of State and Department of Defense. "Memorandum of Agreement Between the Departments of State and Defense on the Protection and Evacuation of U.S. Citizens and Nationals and Designated Other Persons From Threatened Areas Overseas July 1998." http://poems.ses.state/sites/portal/seso/cms/CoMCheck/Multiple%20Content%20

Type%20Library/DOS-DOD%20MOU%20on%20Evacuations.doc (accessed March 8, 2014.)

U.S. Department of State. *12 Foreign Affairs Handbook -1*. Emergency Planning Handbook . Washington DC: Department of State, 2010.

————. "Evacuations and Drawdowns."http://fsi.state.gov/fsi/lms/cmt. (accessed March 8, 2014).

————. "Evacuation Lessons Learned From Arab Spring Posts." http://poems.ses.state/sites/portal/seso/cms/after/Lessons/2011%20State%201213 43%20-%20Lessons%20Learned%20from%20Arab%20Spring%20Posts.doc (accessed March 8, 2014).

————. "Guidance on Drawdown, Evacuation or Suspension of Mission Operations."http://poems.ses.state/sites/portal/seso/cms/during/Post/Guidance%2 0on%20Drawdowns,%20Evacuations%20and%20Suspension%20of%20Operatio ns.docx (accessed March 8, 2014).

————. "Lessons Learned from AMEMB Conakry's Ordered Departure." http://poems.ses.state/sites/portal/seso/cms/after/Lessons/2010%20Conakry%201 73%20-%20Lessons%20Learned,%20Ordered%20Departure.doc (accessed March 8, 2014).

U.S. Government Accountability Office. *Report 07-893R US Evacuation From Lebanon Jun 2007*. Washington DC: Government Accountability Office, June 2007.

————. *Report 08-23 State Department: Evacuation Planning and Preparations for Overseas Posts Can Be Improved*. Washington DC: Government Accountability Office, October 2007.

U.S. Joint Chiefs of Staff. *Noncombatant Emergency and Evacuation (NEMVAC) Lessons Learned Survey*. Collection: U.S. Policy in the Vietnam War, 1969-1975 United States: Joint Chiefs of Staff, May 19, 1975.

U.S. Office of the Chairman of the Joint Chiefs of Staff. *Noncombatant Evacuation Operations*. Joint Publication 3-68. Washington, DC: Joint Chiefs of Staff, December 23, 2010.

Urey, Patrick, W. *U.S. Marine Corps participation in the emergency evacuations of Phnom Penh and Saigon : operations Eagle Pull and Frequent Wind*. Alexandria, VA: Center for Naval Analyses, 1977.

U.S. President. *National Security Strategy of the United States*. Washington DC, Government Printing Office, May 2010.

This page intentionally left blank

VITA

LtCol Stephen M. Kampen most recently served as the Executive Officer of Marine Air Control Group 18 in Okinawa, Japan. Commissioned in 1993 from the Platoon Leaders Course upon graduation from Salisbury State University. Following initial training he reported to Okinawa, Japan and served as a Platoon Commander at First Stinger Battery. He also commanded a battery at Third Low Altitude Air Defense Battalion as well as squadron command at Marine Tactical Air Command Squadron 18. Other operational tours include operations officer at the Battalion and Group levels, deploying to Iraq in support of Operation Iraqi Freedom on three occasions, and in the operations section at Marine Forces Pacific. His supporting establishment tours include Marine Corps Recruit Depot and the Expeditionary Warfare School. Lieutenant Colonel Kampen is a graduate of the USMC Expeditionary Warfare School (Distance Learning) and the USMC Command and Staff College.

This page intentionally left blank

www.ingramcontent.com/pod-product-compliance
Lightning Source LLC
Chambersburg PA
CBHW080542290526

45790CB00006B/2509